Charlie Chaplin

BOOKS BY GLORIA KAMEN

FIORELLO: His Honor, the Little Flower
CHARLIE CHAPLIN: The Little Tramp

by Gloria Kamen

ATHENEUM   NEW YORK   1982

ACKNOWLEDGMENTS

My thanks to The American Film Institute of the
Kennedy Center, The Film Division of The Library of
Congress and to The British Information Services for their
help in researching this book. Special thanks go to
Adam Hubbel and Roger Avery for their assistance with
information on British clog dancing and to J. T. and
T. M. Fleet's book, *Traditional Step-Dancing in Lakeland.*

Library of Congress Cataloging in Publication Data

Kamen, Gloria   Charlie Chaplin.

1. Chaplin, Charlie, 1889-1977-Juvenile literature.
2. Moving-picture actors and actresses—United States—
Biography—Juvenile literature. 3. Comedians—United
States—Biography—Juvenile literature. I. Title.
PN2287.C5K3   791.43'028'0924   82-1674
ISBN 0-689-30925-2   AACR2

To my daughters
Tina, Ruth, and Julie
with love

Contents

Introduction

Back in the days of your grandparents, children used to jump rope or bounce a ball and sing:

> Charlie Chaplin went to France
> To teach the ladies how to dance
> Heel, toe, over we go,
> Heel, toe, over we go.

Who was Charlie Chaplin? He was a master clown of the old silent movies. He was a fine actor, director and a composer of music. During his long life he went from poverty to great wealth. He went from being adored to being hated, to being honored around the world.

The story of Chaplin's life is a long one. I will not try to tell it all. What is important is his work and those things in his life that shaped the artist he became.

1. Alone

He should have noticed. His mother had been acting strangely the last few days. She stared out the window. She didn't smile when he came home. She stopped sewing. There was no food in the house.

Something made him hurry home. As he entered his dingy street the children stopped him at the gate.

"Your mother's gone crazy," said one of them.

"What do you mean?" mumbled Charlie turning pale.

"She's been knocking on doors . . . giving away pieces of coal. Says they are birthday presents for the children. Ask my mother."

So that was it! His mother's mind had snapped . . . again. Twelve-year-old Charlie Chaplin raced upstairs. One look at his mother's vacant face and he knew that what they had told him was true. He ran and buried his head in her lap. When his mother stroked his hair, he burst into tears. All the bitter memories of Hanwell School came flooding back. The last time his mother became ill he was only seven. He was sent to Hanwell School for Orphans and Destitute Children, not knowing what it was like. It was called a school, but Captain Hindrum, the headmaster, ran it like a prison. A vision of the dreary rows of cots, the orphans' uniforms, made him sob even more. Charlie had spent the worst eighteen months of his life there. He would *never go back.*

The landlady had already sent for the parish doctor who was old and grumpy. His examination of Hannah Chaplin was brief. "Insane," he said. "She can't stay here. Best get her to Cane Hill Infirmary."

"She'll get proper food there," the landlady said trying to console Charlie. "She's half starved."

The infirmary was a mile away. There was no way to get there but walk, for not a penny was left in the house. The doctor had not thought of offering them the carfare.

Charlie tried as best he could to support his mother down the three flights of stairs. His mother appeared drunk, swaying from side to side. Hannah, who never touched alcohol, had had nothing to drink . . . or eat . . . that day or the day before. All that was in the house, some tea and a "sweet," she had saved for her son.

After the long, painful walk to the hospital, Hannah was led away by the nurse. The young infirmary doctor turned to Charlie, "And what will become of you, young man?" he asked.

"Oh, I'll be living with my aunt," replied Charlie quickly.

There was no aunt. There was only Charlie's older brother, Sydney. But Sydney was away at sea. Because their father had died two years ago, Sydney, at sixteen, was working as a sailor and was the main support of the family. Their mother's frequent headaches had made it impossible for her to earn enough money by her sewing. The sewing machine, never fully paid for, had been taken away again. The small sums Charlie earned as an errand boy or by giving dancing lessons had helped. But weeks had passed since the last of Sydney's small advance had been spent. They had hoped the thirty-five shillings he gave them when he left would last until he returned, but two months had gone by and he was still away. Then came news that he was ill and sent to a hospital in Cape Town. This was the final blow. Hannah could not face being evicted and sent to the Lambeth Workhouse one more time. It was this that made her mind snap.

After leaving the hospital, Charlie walked the streets of London. Not knowing where else to go, he returned to his empty room on Pownall Terrace.

The landlady felt sorry for Charlie. Until she found a new tenant, she told him, he could stay in their third-floor room. All the same, Charlie planned to keep out of her sight. She might take it into her head to tell the authorities that he was alone, and he would find himself back in Hanwell Orphanage. Somehow, some way, he was determined to take care of himself until Sydney returned. Without Sydney . . . But he did not like to think of that.

Each morning at the first sign of daylight, he crept downstairs. Silently, cautiously, he slipped past the landlady's door into the street. Under a London sky the color of dusty chalk he headed for Kennington Road and the woodcutters' shack. There he spent the day tying sticks into small bundles sold for kindling. The woodcutters, who lived off the tiny sums earned this way, could not afford to pay him. Instead they shared their meal of cheese rinds with him. The kindly grocer filled a bag with leftover rinds in return for the few pennies Charlie placed on the counter. The rinds, melted over the open fire, made a meal for all of them. That, and a few bites of bread, was all Charlie had to eat for the day.

The woodcutters did not know who their young helper was. Charlie did not bother to tell them. He was not the only boy living off the streets. Victorian London had many like him.

Charlie knew he was no ordinary street boy. Dirty and ragged, he looked just like all the others. But to Charlie it seemed just another role, like a part in a play. He had had to be many different boys during his childhood: from the pampered baby of popular entertainers to the sad little orphan at Hanwell.

2. Early Childhood

London of 1889, the year Charles Spencer Chaplin was born, was a huge, bustling city. It was the hub, the center from which ships spread out like spokes of a wheel to circle the globe. Gems, gold, and minerals came from Africa. Silks and spices arrived from India, cotton and tobacco from America. It was a city of mansions and great wealth. It was also a city of grimy slums and poverty.

By the time Charlie was twelve he had had a taste of both sides of London. His mother and father were popular music-hall entertainers when Charlie was born. His mother, who sang under the name Lily Harley, loved to dress him in fancy velvet jackets. As a baby, he was wrapped in a warm rug and deposited backstage while she sang. He was pampered, petted and admired by the other entertainers. Listening from the wings, it wasn't long before he learned to sing all his mother's songs . . . and everyone else's. Life backstage was warm and secure, until the day that Lily Harley's voice failed her. Charlie was five years old at the time.

Charlie's mother and father separated a year after he was born. Hannah Chaplin (Lily Harley's real name) tried to support her two sons singing in noisy theaters and music halls. After a while, her not-so-strong voice failed under the strain. One evening, in the middle of a popular ballad, her voice cracked. The audience booed and hooted. The theater manager panicked. He lifted Charlie, who was watching as usual from the wings, and set him in front of the audience. "Sing!" he commanded.

Charlie did. And with such a perfect imitation of his mother's song that he made his voice crack exactly where hers had.

The audience laughed and applauded. Charlie sang another song and broke into a dance. The audience thought it was all part of the act and showered the stage with coins. When the manager dashed onto the stage to collect the money, Charlie stopped singing. He ran to collect his share. The crowd howled with delight. Hannah did not find it funny. She snatched Charlie into her arms and left. Hannah never performed on the stage again. Despite this sad ending to her own career, Hannah always enjoyed talking to her sons about the pleasures and joys of the theater.

Unable to earn money as a singer, Hannah moved to cheaper rooms and took in sewing. The work was never-ending, it seemed. Still, Hannah managed to make their

flat a warm and pleasant home. She amused the boys by telling made-up stories about the people who walked by their window.

"Look at him. He's had a fight with his wife," she'd say. "Going to the pub for a game of darts. Like to toss one at the old lady, I suspect."

And she would imitate his scowl and angry walk.

It became a game Charlie loved. In turn Charlie did imitations to cheer his mother, who usually rewarded him with a smile and loud applause.

Like sand dribbling through an hourglass, everything Hannah Chaplin owned was soon gone. Even her old costumes were sold or cut up and made into clothes for the boys. Charlie's classmates named him "Sir Francis Drake" when he came to school wearing red stockings made from a pair of his mother's tights.

Meals, too, were "patched together" with whatever food they could afford. When, at last, no amount of patching and scraping helped to provide rent money, Hannah and her sons were sent to the Lambeth Workhouse. London's poorhouse broke Hannah's spirit. She was sent to Cane Hill Asylum; the boys were put in the Hanwell Orphanage. Charlie was only seven, separated for the first time from his brother (who was sent to live with the older boys) and his mother. He was miserable.

After eighteen dreary months, Charlie was returned to Hannah, who had recovered enough to try once more to keep her family together.

Hannah earned so little that both boys left school and went to work. Charlie was lucky. He did not have to work in a factory.

At eight years old Charlie joined a group of clog dancers, "The Eight Lancashire Lads," as they were called. Mr. Jackson, who ran the troupe, had been a friend of Charlie's father. His mother, at first doubtful, finally agreed to let him go on the stage. While Charlie lived and traveled with the troupe, his mother received his weekly salary.

The troupe gave three and four shows a night, which was hard work for the younger dancers. Charlie began to look pale and thin. He was sent home with asthma and had to rest for several months. Poverty closed in once more.

He had turned ten. He had only gone to school a week here and a week there while clog dancing. There seemed no way to catch up now. A scant two years of schooling were not long enough even for a bright child. Charlie could barely read or write.

When he was well again, Charlie worked at many different jobs. He was a page, a janitor, a printer's helper and a dance instructor.

His brother Sydney went to work as a messenger for the telegraph office. At sixteen, he signed up as a bugler on a ship sailing for Africa.

He returned from his first voyage with his pockets bulging with silver coins, tips given him for waiting on tables after blowing the bugle calls for meals. When the next ship was ready to sail he eagerly signed up to go. Only this time he was taken ill and left in South Africa. The ship returned without him.

3. Sydney's Return

At Pownall Terrace the landlady had been waiting all day. As Charlie slipped inside the door after a day with the woodcutters, she waved a telegram in front of him.

"It's for you," she said. Charlie stiffened. Was it bad news?

"Could you read it to me?" Charlie asked.

"Arriving Waterloo Station 10 A.M. Love Sydney."

Charlie's face flushed with excitement and joy. His life on the streets had ended. Sydney was coming home!

At Waterloo Station, the next morning, Charlie's smiling face could not hide the fact that something was wrong. Sydney had never seen his brother so ragged and dirty.

"It's Mother," Charlie finally blurted out. "She's back in Cane Hill Asylum."

With eight words Charlie had erased all the joy of homecoming for Sydney, the joy of giving Hannah the twenty British pounds he had earned on the trip. Together they returned to the room in Pownall Terrace to make plans . . . plans that could no longer include their mother. Sydney had already decided not to return to sea. Now he was sure he needed to stay in London to care for Charlie.

The twenty British pounds (about sixty dollars) was a lot of money in 1900. Food was paid for in pennies, rent and clothing were cheap. If they were careful, they could live on this small fortune for months.

Both brothers talked about becoming actors. Together they haunted the theatrical agencies until they found work. Charlie's only experience was as a clog dancer. Sydney had never been on the stage.

A postcard arrived one day asking Charlie to call on the Blackwell Agency. They had a part for a young boy in a new play called *Sherlock Holmes*. Charlie wanted very badly to be given the role of pageboy in the play. He knew he could do it. He had already "acted it" in real life.

When he came to the theater, everyone agreed he looked just right for the part. They handed him the script. Charlie turned pale. What if they asked him to read his lines? Luckily, they didn't. He was told to take the script home and study it.

Charlie returned home dazed with happiness.

His part in the play was a long one, almost twenty pages. Sydney read the part aloud until his brother had it memorized. In three days Charlie was almost word-perfect. Only one word bothered him: the name *Pierpont Morgan.*

"Who do you think you are—*Putterpint Morgan?*" Charlie said every time.

When he made the mistake at rehearsal the director thought it was funny and made him keep it that way. The play ran successfully for several months.

Sydney also found work in the theater as a comic actor. With their joint earnings they left Pownall Terrace and moved to a better part of London.

The success of *Sherlock Holmes* helped Charlie find other acting roles and his reputation as a boy actor grew.

4. Between Boyhood and Manhood

Performing was in the Chaplin blood. Charlie loved it. Working alongside famous actors in some of the best London theaters was a dream come true. What excitement there was the night the King of Greece came with his three children to see *Sherlock Holmes!*

But there were weeks and months while touring with the show when Charlie was lonely. Everyone in the cast was much older; there was no one his age to talk to. Charlie returned to the boardinghouse each night after the show and went to his room. Unknown to his landlady he once hid a live rabbit under his bed to keep him company.

In every new town and city, he spent his free time

browsing in bookshops. He was teaching himself to read now, at first slowly, but he soon found great pleasure in it. He was discovering history, literature, science . . . all the things he'd missed by leaving school. He still didn't care much for writing and rarely answered Sydney's letters. Sydney too was often away working in smaller theaters around England.

Because he looked younger than he really was, Charlie was able to play boy roles until he was sixteen. But signs of adolescence could not be hidden forever. When he tried out for parts in new plays, he was considered too old for boy parts . . . but not old enough for a man's role.

He found himself out of work.

Lonely, romantic, restless and idle—this was Charlie at seventeen. He tried writing his own play. It failed. He tried a comedy routine, which was booed off the stage. He took up violin. He thought of becoming a violinist instead of an actor.

He fell in love . . . many times . . . with many pretty girls. One of them was Hetty, a lovely showgirl of fifteen who bewitched him. He was madly in love, he thought, and in two weeks he asked her to marry him. She refused. When he tried to see Hetty some years later, he was crushed to hear that she had died. A vision of Hetty as the perfect woman lasted for thirty-five years. She was his model for all the sweet, innocent heroines of his early films. Not until Chaplin was fifty-four did he find his real-life "Hetty" . . . young Oona O'Neil, to whom he remained married until he died.

5. From Acting to Clowning

Every neighborhood in London had its music halls and theaters. They were two of the most popular places of entertainment. Anyone with a few coins to spend could enjoy an evening of singing, dancing, or comedy. Many of the favorite comics of the time used pantomime. Pantomiming or clowning uses the body instead of words to create laughter. A fine pantomimist is an actor, a dancer, an acrobat, and a mimic. He must use every part of his body, except his voice, to express meaning. The history of clowning in Europe goes back to the days of the kings and the court jesters of the middle ages.

The best clowns in Britain at the time Charlie was growing up worked for Fred Karno. He had so many companies he was always in need of new talent. His comedy troupes performed all over Europe and across the Atlantic, in America. Karno had seen Sydney Chaplin act with another troupe and hired him for one of his own.

After Sydney had worked for Karno for some time, he asked if he would give his younger brother a job. For months Karno said no. Charlie was too young. When at last he agreed to meet him, he told Charlie, "Seventeen is very young and you look even younger."

"That," said Charlie, with a shrug of his shoulders, "is a question of make-up."

That shrug, Karno said years later, got Charlie the job.

And so, at seventeen, Charlie Chaplin started to learn the art that would make him world-famous, the art of pantomime.

Once again Charlie needed all his natural talent and ability to learn quickly. He had only one week to learn his part alongside the star of the show, Harry Weldon.

The part was not very exciting, so Charlie added some ideas of his own. His clowning made the audience laugh. This delighted Charlie. But Harry Weldon was not pleased. *He* was the star. He wanted to keep all the best laughs for himself.

One night, instead of a fake punch, Weldon swung hard enough to give Charlie a bloody nose.

"Jealous!" said Charlie as he walked off the stage.

"Why, I have more talent in my arse than you have in your whole body!" replied Weldon.

"That's where your talent lies," was the quick answer.

Weldon and Chaplin never became friends, but Fred Karno recognized Charlie's popularity with the audience. He made plans to send Charlie to Paris and later, across the Atlantic to America.

6. Off to America

Charlie had grown up. He was one of the Karno Company stars after four years of hard work. And now he was leaving for America, perhaps to stay.

At twenty-one he was ready for any new adventure, any change. He bid Sydney goodby in a brief note saying: "Off to America. Will keep you posted. Love, Charlie."

The trip across the Atlantic was rugged. Charlie didn't share his room with a pet rabbit this time . . . but with rats! His ship had carried cattle on the last trip. The cattle were gone but the rats were not.

When, at last, they arrived in New York City, Charlie was excited by the lights of Broadway, the tall buildings and the crowds. The city was alive with newcomers hoping to make their way in a new country. It was his hope as well. But almost no one in New York had heard of Charlie Chaplin. It was just like starting over again.

The Karno Company traveled around the United States for twenty weeks. The tour was not a big success, for British humor was strange to many Americans. Charlie's act, however, an imitation of a gentleman drunk, was popular. After another six weeks in New York, the company left for England. Charlie returned with them, too unsure of himself to remain behind.

But a year later he was back. This tour, like the last one, went to the Midwest, the Pacific Coast, the North and the South. He loved meeting every kind of American: farmers and ranchers, small-town clerks and burly woodsmen, Indians and innkeepers. During the long train rides across country, Charlie spent hours playing his violin or reading. He was considered unfriendly by the rest of the company. He seemed to prefer being alone.

When the Karno Company returned East a strange telegram arrived at the theater where they were performing. It said:

IS THERE A MAN NAMED CHAFFIN IN YOUR

COMPANY OR SOMETHING LIKE THAT STOP

IF SO WILL HE CALL KESSEL AND BAUMAN.

The manager decided it must be for Charlie. There was no one called Chaffin in the company. So Charlie went to see Kessel & Bauman, thinking they were lawyers. He hoped some mysterious, rich aunt had left him a fortune. They were not lawyers but they were the key to his fortune just the same.

7. Silent Movies

When he arrived in New York City, Chaplin was surprised and puzzled to find that the telegram came from a movie agent. Kessel & Bauman were agents for Mack Sennett, who wanted him for his Keystone Comedies. Two years earlier Sennett had seen Chaplin act on the stage and was impressed with his miming. He hadn't remembered his name but he remembered that he wanted him for his movies. Sennett offered to double Charlie's salary if he came to work for him.

Keystone Comedies were very popular. Charlie had seen the Keystone Cops' pie-slinging, slapstick chases in the movies. He didn't think much of them. Was it wise to give up a good stage career for that? Still, the chance to make more money and to try something new was very tempting. He decided to try it for one year. And so, at the end of the tour with Karno, he left for Hollywood.

Chaplin's first glimpse at movie-making was enough to make him wish he hadn't left vaudeville.

The Sennett Studios were in run-down buildings that were once part of a farm. All of Hollywood, in fact, was farmland only a few years earlier.

At the Sennett Studio Lot *five* movies were being made side by side. Five sets, shaded by large linen cloths to keep out the sunlight, were lined up in a row in front of five cameras. Directors and cameramen were giving orders, carpenters were banging props into place, actors were throwing pies, shouting and talking. It sounded like a country fairground. How, wondered Charlie, could he ever concentrate on acting in a setup like that?

Because there was no sound track no one worried about the noise. Only a few years earlier it was even worse. Some studios allowed visitors to watch for twenty-five cents. But the giggles, snickers and comments from the observation platform put a stop to that.

Film-making in 1913, when Chaplin first reported for work, was a squealing, newborn industry. New movie houses were springing up in every town and city. The early two-reelers (a film was shown by reels with interruptions for rewinding) took fifteen minutes to see and only a week to make. Film companies such as Keystone were turning out thirty-five new movies a year. The same sets were used over and over again. Sometimes the picture was made right on the streets and fields of Los Angeles.

There was no time for writing a script. The director made up the story (if there was one) as he went along.

In silent movies actors had no lines to memorize. Instead words for the story were flashed on the screen as titles. The performers pantomimed. Acting was very exaggerated. Everything had to be expressed by gesture and by the actor's face.

Only a few of the early film-makers tried treating movies as an art. For the rest, it was as simple as turning out hamburgers . . . and sold just as well.

All of this changed in just a few years.

Before coming to Hollywood, Charlie had never been in front of a movie camera in his life. What he had just seen on the movie set upset him.

"Is it an acrobatic part?" he asked the director, nervously.

He had just seen another comic fall twenty-five feet into a safety net that broke.

The director assured him it wasn't and sent Chaplin to the dressing room to put on some make-up. He could hardly believe that young Charlie was experienced enough to replace their best comic. Charlie was only twenty-four.

The day's filming started as usual without a script. The story was almost the same as the one they did the week before.

Harry Lehrman, the director, began shouting orders to the actors and crew. Chaplin was nervous. The first day of filming was a disaster.

It didn't take Chaplin long to discover that acting in front of a camera was very different from acting in the theater. After being pushed through a door in one scene he was expected to appear on the other side with the same expression . . . two days later! He kept walking out of camera range, ruining many feet of film. The director was furious!

Lehrman was sure Sennett had made a big mistake in hiring Chaplin. Sennett began to wonder too and asked Charlie to sit on the sidelines and watch for a few days until he understood film-making better.

8. The Tramp

Chaplin was standing in a corner of the movie lot watching Mack Sennett direct a movie. "Put on some comedy make-up," said Sennett, turning to Chaplin. "We need something funny here . . . anything will do."

It was the first time in three weeks anyone had asked him to act.

Charlie entered the dressing room hoping that this time he wouldn't fail, that Sennett would not be disappointed in him.

The costume room looked like a secondhand clothing shop filled with rumpled uniforms, wigs, hats, pants, dresses, and jackets.

Charlie nervously pulled on some baggy old pants, a tight jacket and tie. He picked out shoes so huge that he had to tie them on opposite feet to keep them on. He placed a derby on top of his curly black hair and added a skinny bamboo cane to his outfit, and, to make himself look older, pasted a black mustache under his nose. With a pair of scissors he trimmed the ends so they barely reached the corners of his mouth. He darkened his eyebrows, winked into the mirror and wiggled his mustache. The image in the mirror was not young Chaplin. He had become someone else!

Charlie strutted onto the movie lot swinging his cane. The camera crew, director, and actors turned to watch.

"I had no idea of the character when I entered the dressing room. But the moment I was dressed, it made me feel the person he was. By the time I walked onto the stage," said Charlie, "the Little Tramp was fully born."

Just like the genii who came to Aladdin when he rubbed the magic lamp, Charlie Chaplin had touched some old clothes and a new person magically appeared before him. For Charlie Chaplin, the tramp was real . . . someone outside him. His tramp was a mixture of two people he once knew: the hobo he met who shared a drink and meal with him in Los Angeles one evening and the old cabman he knew on Kennington Road. As a child Charlie had laughed at the cabman's shuffling walk caused by his chronically sore feet. This shuffle became the walk of the little tramp.

Ideas for the tramp went racing through his head. His little "fella" would have the manners of a gentleman mixed with the knavish tricks and swagger of a hobo. He would be romantic, a dreamer, and often, a loser.

Chaplin walked onto the movie lot, tipped his hat to an actress and tripped over a hatrack. He picked himself up, apologizing and tipping his hat to the hatrack, then turned and smiled meekly into the camera. He used his cane like a baton, twirling and bending it. His eyebrows did a little dance above his nose. His walk was a shuffling dance. He added more of his early music hall routine and soon had everyone laughing. Sennett watched until his whole body shook with laughter. This was what Charlie needed most . . . the approval of laughter.

Yes, the tramp *was* funny, but Lehrman didn't see how he fit into the fast-moving, slapstick chases of the Keystone Comedies.

Besides, Lehrman didn't like working with Chaplin, didn't like the slow, studied pantomime he used. All right for the stage, he thought, but *not* for movies.

He was totally wrong. Movies with the little tramp outsold every other Keystone comedy. So when Chaplin refused to work with Lehrman and threatened to quit, Sennett allowed him to direct his own pictures.

Audiences loved Chaplin, the tramp, before they even knew who he was. Names of performers were not given in early movies. The only name to appear on the screen was the name of the company. Film producers feared that once audiences got to know the names of their favorite actors and actresses, it would make a "star" of them. A "star"

would demand more pay. This is, of course, exactly what happened. But there was no way to stop it. Moviegoers and newspapers wanted names, wanted to know who the funny little comic with the toothbrush mustache was.

When a reporter came to interview him one day, Chaplin said, "There's nothing worth talking about. I'm no one . . . just a plain fellow."

"Plain fellow?" Hardly. He was, by then, the most popular comic in movies.

After one year with Mack Sennett, a year in which he learned a great deal about moviemaking, Chaplin no longer thought of returning to the stage.

Before leaving to join a new company, Charlie recommended a good comic to replace him at Keystone—his brother, Sydney. Now it was his turn to help Sydney. Sydney left England for Hollywood and a career in movies. He never became the master comic his younger brother was, nor was he ever as popular. But they often worked together. Sydney took small parts in some of the pictures his brother wrote and directed, and, as in the early days, acted as his brother's business manager.

The earliest films were nothing like the movies we see today. They usually lasted only a few minutes, cameras were primitive, and the photography was very crude. Since the early cameras had to be used in natural light, Southern California became the best place to make movies. Year-round sunshine and a mild climate made it possible to use the camera outdoors almost every day of the year. This, more than any other is the reason Hollywood became the center of film-making.

When movies became longer and required better screens and projectors, special "movie houses" were built. Before that a nickel or a dime would admit you to a viewing "parlor" or a converted music hall set up to show pictures.

Not until World War I did anyone realize how popular movies would become or how much money could be made from them.

Chaplin, more than anyone else, was amazed at his sudden wealth and fame. Chaplin dolls, Chaplin comic strips and posters appeared everywhere. Imitators, calling themselves names like "Charlie Aplin," tried to capture some of his popularity for themselves.

After only three years of making movies Charlie Chaplin was a world-famous star and a millionaire.

Once, when a contest was held in Los Angeles for the best imitation of the little tramp, Chaplin himself joined the thirty contestants. The judges, unaware that the real Chaplin was on the stage, gave him third prize. Charlie enjoyed telling this story to his friends.

9. A New Kind of Comedy

What made Chaplin so popular? It was something more than just the grace with which he used his body. It was the way he expressed feeling and made people *care* about his wistful little tramp.

In movie after movie, Charlie's tramp faced up to the biggest bully on the street or on the job. His zany way of landing a swift kick on the bad guy, then skidding around corners on one foot with the other pointing out like a railroad flag was funny. But there was something more to it. He was acting out a common dream: outsmarting the bully. His movies poked fun at the rich and made the proud and pompous look absurd.

Charlie Chaplin knew from his childhood how helpless and frightened many people feel, how much sadness was mixed with laughter.

When, in his movie, the tramp loses his job and loses his girl, we feel sad. But something about the way he hikes up his pants, shrugs his shoulders and twirls his cane as he walks down the road seems to say things are going to be better next time.

As someone once said, Chaplin movies put a lump in your throat . . . and then make you cough it up with a laugh.

Chaplin believed that comedy was the hardest kind of acting. To be good, a comedian had to understand human nature. As Chaplin put it, "Comedy must be real and true to life. When things get bad enough," he said, "they become funny."

Trouble with the landlady, the boss, the new job, even hunger and war, were the subjects of his best and funniest films.

During his second and third year of film-making he didn't always play "the tramp." In one movie he dressed as a woman. In another he used the story of the opera, *Carmen,* to do a comic version of Don José, the handsome soldier. Charlie called his Spanish soldier "Darn Hosiery." But afterwards he always returned to the character of the little tramp. It remained his best movie role.

Each year he made fewer movies. The more popular his movies became, the harder he worked to make them better. Some said he was never satisfied, impossible to please. At times he had his crews at the end of their patience and the leading lady in tears.

"We rehearsed over fifty times some of the small situations in a movie," said Chaplin. "A little twist of the foot on a ladder, or dropping a bag of meal on a man's head took hours of time."

Picture the poor actor on whose head that bag was dropped! And this for only a tiny, momentary laugh in the final film. No doubt it was Chaplin's foot that climbed the ladder fifty times. Directing *and* acting, he worked harder than anyone else.

Success brought other problems. His life away from the studio was no longer private. Each small detail of his life was written up and talked about. It was like living in a glass cage.

"What difference does it make whether I eat mustard with my ice cream or put sugar in beer," said a distressed Chaplin, "except on the screen?"

But the public wanted to know more and more about the man behind the clown. More stories were written about movie stars than presidents or prime ministers. The pressure of work, too much publicity and a difficult personality had already caused Chaplin's two marriages to break up. He wanted quiet and the privacy in which to work. Each new movie left him exhausted. Not only was he the star but he was also the director, the writer and the producer. Chaplin had *too many talents*. He would not allow others to do any of the planning or writing for him. He did not take advice, trusting only his own feelings. Every detail of his film, from choosing the stars to picking the music and sets, he did himself. Later, he even wrote the music to go with his pictures. Work started at daybreak and ended late at night. Sometimes he fell asleep in his clothes, too tired to get undressed.

When World War I broke out in 1914, American movies, especially Chaplin's were more in demand than ever all over the world. Charlie, Charlot, Carlos, Carlito—whatever they called him—could take their mind off the war.

The war went on for four years. Thousands were killed and crippled. Poison gas and life in mud-filled trenches made some go mad. There was so much tragedy and so little reason to laugh.

When the United States entered the war, Chaplin traveled around the country selling war bonds and entertaining troops. After his third tour he started work on a movie about the life of a poor soldier in the trenches. He called it *Shoulder Arms*. He wasn't sure how people would feel about using the recent war as a subject for comedy. But his story of the sad soldier who never gets mail, who sleeps in a bunk two feet under water by using a phonograph horn and tube as a snorkel was a great success. By the time the movie was finished the war was nearly over. People could laugh about the miseries they had been through. Once again Chaplin showed how close laughter is to tears.

He did the same in the movie, *The Kid*. In some ways the story of *The Kid*, about an orphan boy, reflected his own life as a child. It was both very sad and very funny. Movie theaters were filled to capacity wherever it was shown.

While many stories Chaplin wrote for his movies came from his own experience, others did not.

Sometimes the idea came from a bit of music, a sad-looking dog or something he read. With the movie, *The Gold Rush*, it came unexpectedly from an old photo. It was a picture of the snow-covered Chilkoot Pass in Alaska. Chaplin peered at the long line of prospectors climbing the Pass during the Klondike Gold Rush. He could picture the little tramp somewhere in that long line. He could see him battling blizzards and big, tough prospectors, wistfully dreaming of striking gold.

Something else clicked into place. He remembered the story he had just read about a group of pioneers on their way to California. Most of them died when they lost their way in the Sierra Nevada Mountains. Some of the eighteen survivors told how, in desperation, they roasted their moccasins to relieve their hunger. Once more, a real-life tragedy became the source of wonderful comedy.

A copy of Chilkoot Pass was built in the snow-covered mountains of Nevada. Inside a tiny cabin in the midst of a blizzard we see the tramp sitting alone at a rough wooden table. In front of him is his boiled shoe. In silent pantomine, Charlie takes up his knife and fork, a napkin on his lap, and starts to carve away at the shoe. He carefully picks out the nails as though they were the bones of a fish. Then, with a piece of leather in his mouth, chomps away. Next, he winds the shoelaces like spaghetti around his fork and looks for all the world as if he were enjoying a delicious meal.

His companion, Big Jim, is also starving. Looking through famished eyes, Jim sees Charlie turn into a chicken. There on the screen is Charlie dressed in feathers running around the cabin squawking and flapping his arms as Big Jim chases him with a knife.

The saddest scene in the movie shows the tramp alone and friendless on New Year's Eve. He has prepared an elegant meal for two dance-hall girls who never show up. His shirt is the tablecloth. By folding the sleeves in a special way, he makes them look like fancy table napkins. When no one comes, he sadly shuffles along in the snow to the dance hall. There he sees his friends having a good time. They had forgotten about him.

Chaplin considered *The Gold Rush* his best movie.

10. The End of Silent Movies

Charlie Chaplin was ill when *The Gold Rush* was finished. It had taken fourteen months of hard work to finish it. He did not start another film until a year later. *The Circus,* made in 1928, won one of Hollywood's first Academy Awards. Chaplin thought so little of his "Oscar" at the time that he used the gold-plated statue as a doorstop. He did not believe in being judged by other film-makers, he said. His reward came from the audience.

There were long delays after each of his next three pictures. Important changes were taking place. The silent movie days were ending. Movies could now be made to "talk." The first movie made with a sound track caused a lot of excitement. For the first time people talked and sang in *The Jazz Singer.*

For Charlie Chaplin, the prince of pantomime, talking movies seemed to mean the end of his acting career and the end of his little tramp. The tramp appealed to all just because he *had no language* and *no nationality*. To give him a voice, thought Chaplin, was to destroy him. It was like having to face the death of an old friend. So, in 1928, when other film-makers were hurrying to make their own talking movie, Chaplin could not make up his mind what to do.

He began writing a new movie . . . and decided that he could not give up the tramp. So, *City Lights,* the story of a blind flower girl and a penniless tramp who falls in love with her was begun. It was the only silent movie made in Hollywood in 1929. By the time it was finished so many movie houses were wired for sound that Chaplin wrote a musical score to go with the film.

City Lights was his first movie in three years. Would the audience still accept his silent pantomime? Would they come to see another tragic comedy, for this movie more than any other, ended very sadly.

Opening night was a torment . . . until the laughter and applause gave him the answer he hoped for. A New York newspaper wrote, "This morning there is good news. Chaplin is back again."

Chaplin hadn't lost his popularity. When the picture opened in London, he decided to go. It had been many years since he walked the streets of his childhood. He wanted to revisit the places where he and his mother had lived. Hannah had died during the filming of *City Lights*.

Taking time off from a round of parties and interviews Chaplin also visited Hanwell. It was still used as an orphanage. He remembered the sad Christmas at Hanwell School when he wasn't given his orange or Christmas "sweet" because he forgot to make his bed that morning. A movie projector and gifts of toys, oranges and candy for each child arrived at the school the next day.

He left London and continued on a world tour for the next fifteen months. There was no need to hurry back. He believed he had made his last film.

11. Modern Times

Hollywood was grinding out sound movies as fast as they could be made. Stars of the silent film drifted out of sight and new stars were created by a new kind of acting. A good voice was important.

Many critics agreed that Chaplin's career had ended. They guessed that his voice wasn't good, that this was why he stopped making pictures. It was not the reason. Chaplin did not want to risk making a bad movie. Every story idea seemed not good enough. It was better to make no movie than a bad one, for movie-making had become very expensive. Sets costing almost half a million dollars were common. They were used to create the new realism expected in pictures.

It was not until Chaplin met and fell in love with a young actress named Paulette Goddard that he started to work on a new film. She was to be the star.

He decided to do a movie about how life had changed for the ordinary working man. Workers had moved from farms to factories in large numbers. No longer were the factories the gray, dingy places of his childhood. In the United States, Henry Ford had built the modern assembly line with its bright, new machinery. Was it better for the men and women who worked on it? Charlie Chaplin felt he had something to say about this. And what he had to say in his movie, *Modern Times,* made some people laugh, some cheer and others . . . become angry.

Modern Times starts with the camera following a herd of sheep pouring through a stockyard gate. The next scene shows factory workers pouring into a factory yard. Inside, the movie focuses on a poor factory worker (Charlie) forced to work faster and faster every time the boss speeds up the machinery. He is constantly losing the fight to keep up with the machines and finally goes crazy. After being cured, he sets up house in a run-down shack with Paulette, a homeless waif. She helps him find a new job in a cafe as a singing waiter. Suddenly, Charlie's voice is heard for the first time ever in movies . . . singing a song. Until then, the picture is silent. His voice is crisp and clear . . . but the words sound foreign. The joke is on the audience. The tramp *has no language.* The words are made-up gibberish. And the pantomime that goes with them is pure Chaplin fun.

The movie ends happily with Paulette and Charlie walking hand-in-hand down a dirt road. In real life they married some time later.

Despite the name, *Modern Times* was not a modern movie. "Talkies" had been out for nine years when the movie opened in 1936. The little tramp looked exactly the same as in 1915. Nevertheless, the movie had original ideas and enough Chaplin surprises to make it a huge success.

The movie career of the tramp ended with *Modern Times*. Chaplin had kept him alive for longer than anyone thought possible.

A new Chaplin, one who talked and acted, appeared in a movie made four years later. The movie was *The Great Dictator* made in 1940 at the start of the Second World War. Adenoid Hynkel, Charlie's role, was a double for Adolph Hitler, the dictator of Nazi Germany. Charlie needed only to dress in uniform, brush his hair over his forehead and walk in a pompous way to resemble Hitler. Hitler wore a toothbrush mustache and was the same size and age as Chaplin.

The movie and Chaplin were warmly applauded. It seemed his career in "talkies" could continue for as long as he wished.

But with his next movie, *Monsieur Verdoux,* everything changed.

12. Unhappy Endings

During the 1930s the world plunged into a great depression. Unemployment, and bitter strikes caused new fear and distrust. World War II and the atom bomb added to these fears. The whole mood of America changed.

Now, instead of kind praise, Chaplin was criticized for being un-American. Why, after so many years of living in the United States did he not become an American citizen, he was asked. His answer did not please his critics.

"Most Americans had gotten their citizenship as an accident of birth," said Chaplin. That he was British was also an "accident of where he had been born." He considered himself a citizen of the world first of all.

He was called a communist. Rumors spread that he did not pay taxes in the United States and had not supported his mother. They were all false he said over and over again. But the stories continued.

He was criticized for his many marriages. When his marriage to Paulette Goddard ended in divorce, Charlie, now fifty-seven, married young Oona O'Neil, who resembled Hetty, his boyhood ideal. Oona, the daughter of a famous playwright, wanted to be an actress. She tried out for a role in a Chaplin movie but traded an acting career for a lifetime part as Charlie Chaplin's wife. Geraldine, their daughter, later took up the career her mother had abandoned.

Most hurtful of all the criticism was the attack on his art. His newest film, *Monsieur Verdoux*, was called a bad movie, not fit to be shown in neighborhood theaters. *Monsieur Verdoux* is the story of a bluebeard, a killer. It was a shocking subject for the 1940s, and some theater owners refused to show the film. The ending of the movie offended many people. Verdoux, about to be hung, refuses to pray with the priest. "War," says the killer, "is the greatest crime." By comparison, Verdoux says, his crimes are unimportant. He walks stiffly to his death seeming to accept his punishment proudly.

Angry voices denounced Chaplin and his movie. Chaplin found it hard to concentrate on his work. He had started a new movie, which had nothing to do with war, religion, or politics. The movie, called *Limelight,* was a very personal movie for Chaplin. It was the story of the life of an old music-hall entertainer.

Many of his family and old friends had small parts. His oldest son, Sydney, had a leading role. Charles, Jr. had the part of a clown. Geraldine, Michael and Josephine Chaplin, still small children, appeared in the opening scene watching an organ grinder in the street as Charlie walks by. Sixty-year-old Chaplin had the main role of an alcoholic, middle-aged entertainer. Chaplin's hair is white and he no longer wears a mustache.

Chaplin left with his family for England as soon as *Limelight* was finished. He decided not to return to America until the criticism and ugly stories about him had stopped.

13. Happy Endings

But the stories did not stop. In anger, he decided never to return to the United States.

Chaplin went to live in a small town in Switzerland, a wealthy and respected man. For the first time in his life he was able to enjoy a quiet family life. He spent his time with Oona and their growing family. Their busy household included eight children and many servants. His oldest sons, Charles and Sydney, were grown up and living elsewhere. In all, Chaplin had ten children.

During his years in Switzerland Chaplin avoided publicity. He was growing old. But he was not forgotten, because his movies were shown over and over again. A whole new generation laughed and fell in love with his little tramp. His native Britain had given him a title. He was called Sir Charles Chaplin after being knighted by the Queen of England.

Then, when his life was nearly over, Chaplin finally received the love and affection of America one more time. It came first from those in the movie industry who still admired his work.

Just before his eighty-third birthday, Charlie Chaplin was invited to the United States to receive a special Academy Award. It was given to him not for any one movie, but for his lifelong work in film-making. Chaplin's fifty years in film and his ninety-six movies had become part of the history of moving pictures, and his famous character was known world-wide.

He returned to the United States with Oona in April, 1972, a frail, white-haired and happy man. It had taken America twenty years to welcome him back.

On Christmas Day, 1977, Charlie Chaplin, the creator of The Little Tramp died in Switzerland. But the other self, The Little Tramp of the movies, lives on.

Bibliography

Chaplin, Charles. *My Autobiography.* New York: Simon & Schuster, Inc., 1964.

Chaplin, Charles, Jr. & Rau, N. & M. *My Father Charlie Chaplin*. London: Longman Green and Co., Ltd. 1960.

Cotes, Peter & Niklaus, Thelma. *The Little Fellow*. London: The Bodley Head, 1951.

Eastman, Max. *Enjoyment of Laughter*. New York: Simon & Schuster, Inc., 1936.

Gifford, Denis. *Chaplin*. New York: Doubleday & Co., Inc., 1974.

Huff, Theodore. *Charlie Chaplin*. New York: Henry Schuman, 1951.

Krows, Arthur Edwin. *The Talkies*. New York: Henry Holt & Co., 1930.

Manvell, Roger. *Chaplin*. Boston: Litlte, Brown & Co., 1974.

Taylor, Deems. *A Pictorial History of the Movies*. New York: Simon & Schuster, Inc., 1945.

Tyler, Parker. *Chaplin: Last of the Clowns*. New York: Vanguard Press, Inc., 1947.

Films of Charlie Chaplin

KEYSTONE STUDIOS (1913-1914—35 one-reel comedies)

AS ACTOR:

Making a Living
Kid Auto Races at Venice
  (the Little Tramp was
  introduced here)
Mabel's Strange Predicament
Between Showers
A Film Johnnie
Tango Tangles

His Favorite Pastime
Cruel Cruel Love
The Star Boarder
Mabel at the Wheel
Twenty Minutes of Love
The Knockout
Tillie's Punctured Romance

AS ACTOR-DIRECTOR:

Caught in a Cabaret
Caught in the Rain
A Busy Day
The Fatal Mallet
Her Friend the Bandit
Mabel's Busy Day
Mabel's Married Life
Laughing Gas
The Property Man
The Face on the Barroom Floor
Recreation

The Masquerader
His New Profession
The Rounders
The New Janitor
Those Love Pangs
Dough and Dynamite
Gentlemen of Nerve
His Musical Career
His Trysting Place
Getting Acquainted
His Prehistoric Past

ESSANAY COMPANY (1915-1916—14 one-reel comedies)

1915:

His New Job
A Night Out
The Champion
In the Park
A Jitney Elopement
The Tramp

By the Sea
Work
A Woman
The Bark
Shanghaied
A Night in the Show

1916:   *Carmen*   *Police*

ALSO-1918:

Triple Trouble (composed of old, unused Chaplin material)

MUTUAL COMPANY (1916-1917)

The Floorwalker	*The Pawnshop*
The Fireman	*Easy Street*
The Vagabond	*The Cure*
One A.M.	*The Immigrant*
The Count	*The Adventurer*

FIRST NATIONAL FILMS (producer)
for Chaplin's own studio (1918-1923)

1918:   *A Dog's Life*   *Shoulder Arms*
The Bond (propaganda film for Liberty Loan)

1919:   *Sunnyside*   *A Day's Pleasure*

1921:   *The Nut* (cameo in Fairbanks film)
The Kid   *The Idle Class*

1922:   *Payday*

1923:   *The Pilgrim*

UNITED ARTISTS (1923-1967)

A Woman of Paris (produced and played cameo—1923)

The Gold Rush (1925)	*Monsieur Verdoux* (1947)
The Circus (1928)	*Limelight* (1952)
City Lights (1931)	*A King in New York* (1957)
Modern Times (1936)	*A Countess from Hong Kong* (1967)
The Great Dictator (1940)	